3 9082 10443 9883

W9-CVA-245

OCEANS ALIVE

Clown Fish

by Colleen Sexton

BELLWETHER MEDIA · MINNEAPOLIS, MN

Note to Librarians, Teachers, and Parents:

Blastoff! Readers are carefully developed by literacy experts and combine standards-based content with developmentally appropriate text.

Level 1 provides the most support through repetition of high-frequency words, light text, predictable sentence patterns, and strong visual support.

Level 2 offers early readers a bit more challenge through varied simple sentences, increased text load, and less repetition of high-frequency words.

Level 3 advances early-fluent readers toward fluency through increased text and concept load, less reliance on visuals, longer sentences, and more literary language.

Whichever book is right for your reader, Blastoff! Readers are the perfect books to build confidence and encourage a love of reading that will last a lifetime!

This edition first published in 2007 by Bellwether Media.

No part of this publication may be reproduced in whole or in part without written permission of the publisher. For information regarding permission, write to Bellwether Media Inc., Attention: Permissions Department, Post Office Box 1C, Minnetonka, MN 55345-9998.

Library of Congress Cataloging-in-Publication Data
Sexton, Colleen A.
  Clown fish / by Colleen Sexton.
    p. cm. — (Oceans alive)
Summary: "Simple text and supportive full-color photographs introduce beginning readers to clown fish. Intended for kindergarten through third grade students"—Provided by publisher.
  Includes bibliographical references and index.
  ISBN-13: 978-1-60014-054-9 (hardcover : alk. paper)
  ISBN-10: 1-60014-054-8 (hardcover : alk. paper)
  1. Anemonefishes—Juvenile literature. I. Title.

QL638.P77S49 2007
597'.72—dc22   2006035210

Contents

Clown fish are small fish.
They are smaller than
your hand.

Clown fish live in warm parts
of the **ocean**. They live near
the ocean floor.

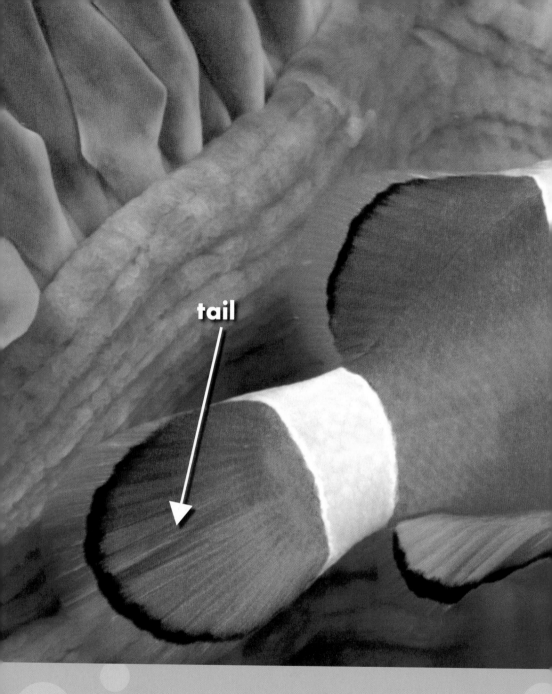

tail

Clown fish have a tail.
They move their tail back
and forth to swim.

fins

Clown fish have rounded **fins**. Clown fish use their bottom fins to steer.

7

Most clown fish are orange
with three white stripes.

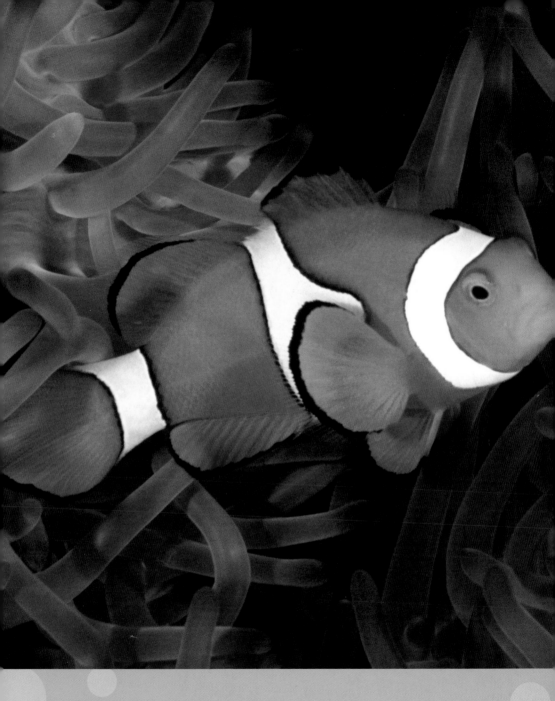

Most clown fish have black
tips on their fins and their tail.

gills

Clown fish have **gills**.
Fish use gills to breathe
in water.

Clown fish have **scales** covering their skin.

Clown fish live with **sea anemones**.

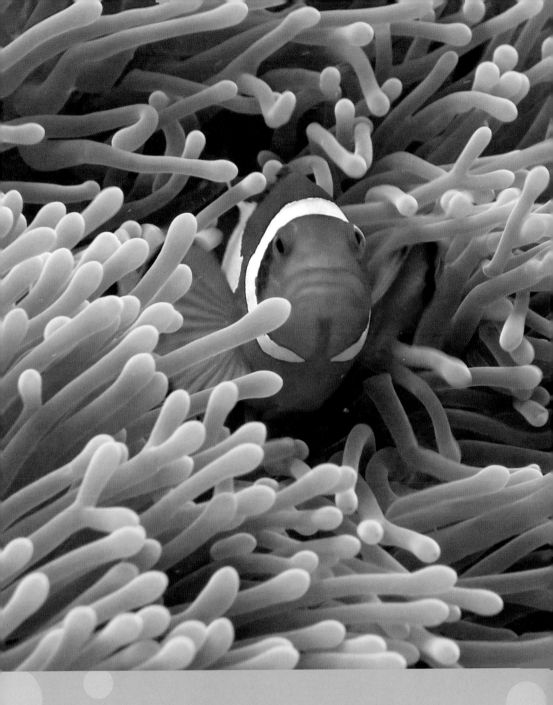

Sea anemones have long **tentacles**.

The tentacles of a sea anemone sting other animals. But they do not hurt the clown fish.

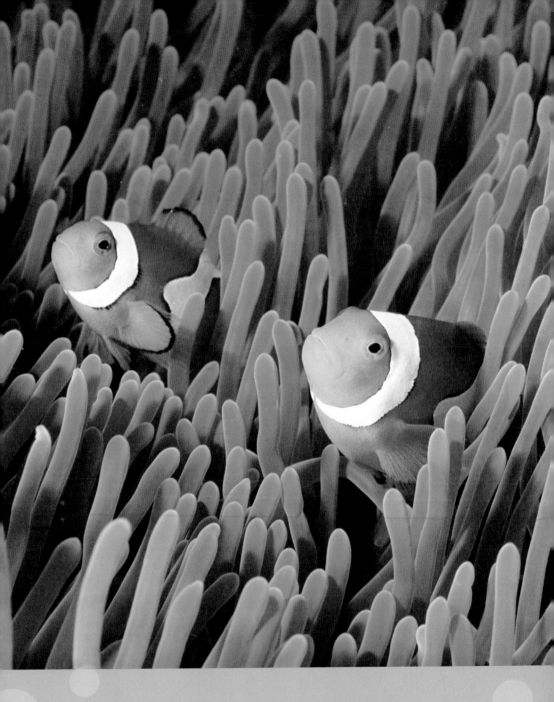

Clown fish have **slime** on their body. The slime **protects** them from stings.

Clown fish and the sea anemone help each other.

Bigger fish try to eat clown
fish. Sea anemones hide
clown fish from other fish.

Clown fish chase away
other fish that want to
eat sea anemones.

Sea anemones use their
tentacles to catch fish
for food.

Clown fish eat the leftovers.
That keeps sea anemones
clean.

20

Clown fish never go far
away from the sea anemone.

Glossary

fins—flaps on a fish's body used for moving and steering through the water

gills—slits near the mouth that a fish uses to breathe; the gills move oxygen from the water to the fish's blood.

ocean—a large body of salty water; clown fish live near coral reefs and rocky reefs in the Indian Ocean and the Pacific Ocean.

protects—to keep safe from harm

scales—hard plates that cover the body of a fish

sea anemone—an ocean animal with a body shaped like a tube and a mouth surrounded by tentacles; sea anemones attach themselves to rocks, coral reefs, and other hard places.

slime—a clear, slippery liquid that covers the body of the clown fish

tentacles—the arms of some ocean animals that are used for catching food; a sea anemone's tentacles have stinging cells that shoot out to sting prey.

To Learn More

AT THE LIBRARY

Johnson, Rebecca. *Clown Fish Finds a Friend*. Milwaukee, Wisc.: Gareth Stevens, 2005.

Lindeen, Carol K. *Clown Fish*. Mankato, Minn.: Pebble Books, 2005.

Maddern, Eric, and Adrienne Kenaway. *Curious Clownfish*. Boston: Little, Brown, and Co., 1990.

Stille, Darlene. *I Am a Fish: The Life of a Clown Fish*. Minneapolis, Minn.: Picture Window Books, 2005.

ON THE WEB

Learning more about clown fish is as easy as 1, 2, 3.

1. Go to www.factsurfer.com

2. Enter "clown fish" into search box.

3. Click the "Surf" button and you will see a list of related web sites.

With factsurfer.com, finding more information is just a click away.

Index

The photographs in this book are reproduced through the courtesy of: Jeff Hunter/Getty Images, front cover, p. 8; Duard van der Westhuizen, pp. 4-5; David Fleetham/Alamy, pp. 6-7, 21; Carlos Villoch/imagequestmarine.com, p. 9; Cousteau Society/Getty Images, p. 10; EcoPrint, p. 11; Jane Gould/Alamy, p. 12; Andy Lim, p. 13, Kasia, p. 14: Stephen Frink/Getty Images, pp. 15, 16-17; Darryl Torckler/Getty Images, p. 18; A. Witte/C. Mahaney/Getty Images, p. 19; Reinhard Dirscherl/Alamy, p. 20.